the Hamster

A guide to selection, housing, care,

nutrition, behaviour, health, breeding,

species and colours

Contents

Foreword 4

In general 6
   Description 6
   History 7
   Fauna falsification 9
   Rodents 9

Buying a hamster 14
   One or more? 15
   Where to buy 15
   Things to watch out for 16
   Selling young hamsters 17
   Catching and handling 18
   Transport 19

Feeding your hamster 20
   Feeding in the wild 20
   Feeding in captivity 20
   Pressed pellets 21
   Vegetables 22
   Fruit 23
   Eating droppings 23
   Vitamins and minerals 23
   Water 23

A home for your hamster 24
   In the wild 24
   Hamster architecture 24
   Housing in captivity 25
   Types of cages 25
   The interior 29
   The best place 31

Behaviour 32
   Scents, sounds and body-talk 32
   House-training 33
   Cuddling your hamster 33
   Taming the hamster 34

Shows 36
   Colours and hairstyles 36

Dwarf hamsters 40
   The Dwarf Russian Hamster 40
   The Campbell's Russian Hamster 41
   The Roborovski Hamster 43
   The Chinese Hamster 45
   One or more? 46
   Which species? 47

Reproduction 48
   Male or female? 48
   Pairing 48
   In-breeding 49
   Mating 49
   Pregnancy and birth 50
   Development 51

Your hamster's health 52
   Prevention 52
   Colds and pneumonia 52
   Diarrhoea 53
   Wet tail 55
   Tumours 55
   Bite wounds 55
   Broken bones 56
   Broken teeth 57
   Overgrown teeth 57
   Malnutrition ailments 57
   Parasites 57
   Skin mites 58
   Fungal skin infections 59
   Old age 59

Clubs 60

Internet 62

Profile 64

Foreword

If you're planning to buy a pet, you should get plenty
of information before doing so, even if it's a small
animal such as the hamster. Is the animal right for
your family? How much work is associated with
caring for it, and how much will that cost? Can you
cuddle it or only view it from a safe distance?

This book will give you an overview of hamster
species kept as pets in Western Europe. It discusses
their characters and needs in detail, as well as their
needs in terms of food and care. A hamster kept
according to its needs is an affectionate housemate
for the young and old. These animals have turned
more than a few people into enthusiastic hobby
breeders.

About Pets

about pets

A Publication of About Pets.

Copyright © 2003
About Pets
co-publisher United Kingdom
Kingdom Books
PO9 5TL, England

ISBN 1852792159
First printing: September 2003
Second printing: June 2005

Original title: *de hamster*
© 1999 - 2005 Welzo Media
Productions bv,
About Pets bv,
Warffum, the Netherlands
http://www.aboutpets.info

Photos:
Rob Dekker,
Rob Doolaard,, Lydia Donkersteeg
Kingdom Books and Dick Hamer,

Printed in China through Printworks Int. Ltd.

In general

The hamster has been a favourite pet for children for many years, and for good reason. Hamsters are especially friendly and affectionate and have a lovely soft coat. They don't "smell" and are inexpensive to buy and keep.

Dwarf Campbell's Russian hamster

The hamster described in this book used to be known as the Golden Hamster because of its golden-brown coat. Today they're found in many different colours, which makes the name "Syrian Hamster" more appropriate. The animal originally came from Syria and the name "hamster" comes from the German word "hamstern" meaning "to hoard", which is its favourite activity and its life. In size and shape the Syrian Hamster fits somewhere between the smaller dwarf hamster and the European Hamster, which is found in the wild in parts of central Europe and can be 25 to 35 cm in size.

Description

A hamster cannot really be compared with any other rodent.

It's plumper and slower than a mouse, softer and more active than a guinea pig or rat, and can happily stand on its rear paws.

Its body is short, wide and stocky, twelve to sixteen centimetres long. Its round head carries a wide blunt snout and its eyes are like large balls. If you pick up a hamster by the scruff of its neck, its eyes will look like they may pop out of their sockets any moment. It has large, round, upright ears. One characteristic of the hamster is, of course, its cheek pouches, which it uses to transport all sorts of things. In proportion to its body, its fore and rear paws are very small. The "hands" on its fore-paws have four little "fingers" and a rudimentary (not fully developed) thumb. Its rear paws have five little "toes" and it has a tail about one centimetre long.

History

Almost all rodents can easily be spotted in the wild, but the Syrian Hamster is rather an exception. In their original habitat, these animals live several metres under the desert surface and rarely appear in the open. Perhaps for that reason they have a fascinating history, of which there are different versions. The most plausible version tells the following tale: In 1797, the existence of the Syrian Hamster was first recorded in the book 'The Natural History of Aleppo'. The town of Aleppo is nowadays known as Habab and lies in the north of Syria, close to the Turkish border.

The English natural scientist Robert Waterhouse was the first to describe the Syrian Hamster scientifically and he gave it the Latin name *Mesocrisetus auratus*. This was in 1839 after he saw a stuffed example in a Beirut museum. "This variety is smaller than the Common (European) Hamster and its deep golden colour is striking", he wrote.

The first scientist to succeed in getting his hands on a live hamster was the Israeli professor Israel Aharoni of the University of Jerusalem. He excavated a nest with a female and twelve young in the region of Aleppo. The young could only have been a few days old as they measured three centimetres. Professor Aharoni succeeded in keeping the mother and some of her young alive. He fed them various seeds, cucumber, bread and meat. In time, one of the young females bore six, then eight and finally even ten young. This group of hamsters turned out to be extremely fertile. Within one year there were some 150 offspring, and almost all hamsters in the world today are descendants of this one group. From laboratories and zoos in Israel, London and the United States, these animals spread across the globe. Hamsters were caught again in Syria in 1971, 1978 and during the eighties. This is certainly proof that the animals are not extinct in the wild, but scientists have no idea exactly how many animals are to be found in the deserts of the Middle East.

Fauna falsification

Syrian Hamsters also live wild in Europe, against all the laws of nature. These are pets that have escaped or been set free. Letting pets escape or setting them free into a habitat that is not their own is a serious form of fauna falsification. These animals can introduce sicknesses or force other animals away from their habitat. There are many known examples of this happening.

Golden Hamster

Common (European) Hamster

It is not only harmful to nature to set a hamster free, but it is also cruel. Of all pets set free, 95 percent starve or die of exhaustion.

At the moment, there are several known populations of Syrian Hamsters in Europe; in England, Holland, Belgium, Germany and Poland among other countries. They live in various types of landscape, with a preference for sandy areas with light vegetation and shrubs.

Rodents

Hamsters are rodents and as such are mammals, just like humans, dogs and horses. Rodents actually form the largest group of mammals; of all the species of mammals in the world, more than half are rodents. The best-known rodents are probably mice and rats, but in fact they come in all shapes and sizes. The largest rodent in the world is the Capybara, or "water pig", which can grow to over a metre long and weigh up to sixty kilos. The tiny tot among the rodents is the African Dwarf Mouse, which is never longer than three centimetres. Between these extremes one finds the squirrel, the guinea pig, the porcupine, marmot, gerbil and countless others. Contrary to popular opinion, rabbits and hares are not rodents. They are more closely related to hoofed animals, such as

the goat. But rabbits and hares do share one significant characteristic with the rodents: they have continuously growing front teeth without roots. Because rodents are constantly gnawing, they grind their front teeth down. Nature found a solution by having their teeth just keep growing. However, rodents do run the risk of so-called "overgrown teeth" and you can read more about that in the chapter on "Your hamster's health". When choosing a cage or a hutch, remember that rodents have sharp teeth and can easily gnaw a hole in wood.

Rodents are very suitable as family pets as they adapt easily to different situations. Generally they are not a threatened species and in fact, in their original habitats, they're often regarded as a pest. But the Syrian Hamster is not found in populated areas.

A family tree can help to show the position that rodents (and thus hamsters) occupy in the animal hierarchy. All existing animals were first divided into two groups: vertebrates and non-vertebrates. The vertebrates have hard body parts, such as bones and teeth, and are in turn divided into five classes: fish, amphibians, reptiles, birds and mammals. The latter, of course, were named "the higher species". The mammals class is again divided into various orders. There is the order of predators, which apart from bears and tigers also

Greater Egyptian Jerboa

African Dormice

Vole

Gerbil

Dwarf Russian
Hamster

includes dogs and cats. The whales fall under a special order. Contrary to what many believe, these animals do not belong in the fish class because their young are born alive. The apes belong to the primate order, while a kangaroo comes under the marsupials. And rodents have their own order, in Latin called *Rodentia* (wherefore the English word "rodent"). As we already said, rabbits and hares do not come under the rodents, they have their own order, the *Lagomorpha*.

The rodent order is then divided into four sub-orders: mice, squirrels, porcupines and guinea pig species. All rats, mice, gerbils and (dwarf) hamsters belong to the sub-order of the mice. This sub-order of the mice is then again divided into three families: real mice, dormice and jumping mice. The family of the real mice is split into three families: hamsters and voles, mice and rats and blind mice (a kind of small mole). The hamster and vole sub-family has five genera: real hamsters, Madagascar rats, maned rats, voles and gerbils (or desert rats). Naturally, the Syrian Hamster belongs to the family of real hamsters, together with the European Hamster and the dwarf hamsters.

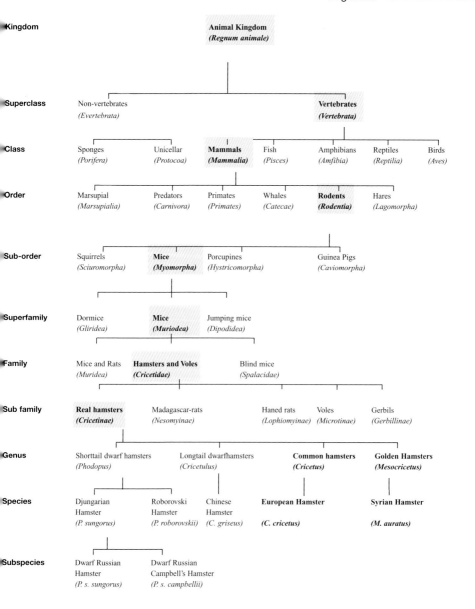

Kingdom	**Animal Kingdom** *(Regnum animale)*					
Superclass	Non-vertebrates *(Evertebrata)*		**Vertebrates** *(Vertebrata)*			
Class	Sponges *(Porifera)*	Unicellar *(Protocoa)*	**Mammals** *(Mammalia)*	Fish *(Pisces)*	Amphibians *(Amfibia)*	Reptiles *(Reptilia)* — Birds *(Aves)*
Order	Marsupial *(Marsupialia)*	Predators *(Carnivora)*	Primates *(Primates)*	Whales *(Catecae)*	**Rodents** *(Rodentia)*	Hares *(Lagomorpha)*
Sub-order	Squirrels *(Sciuromorpha)*	**Mice** *(Myomorpha)*	Porcupines *(Hystricomorpha)*		Guinea Pigs *(Caviomorpha)*	
Superfamily	Dormice *(Gliridea)*	**Mice** *(Muriodea)*	Jumping mice *(Dipodidea)*			
Family	Mice and Rats *(Muridea)*	**Hamsters and Voles** *(Cricetidae)*	Blind mice *(Spalacidae)*			
Sub family	**Real hamsters** *(Cricetinae)*	Madagascar-rats *(Nesomyinae)*	Haned rats *(Lophiomyinae)*	Voles *(Microtinae)*	Gerbils *(Gerbillinae)*	
Genus	Shorttail dwarf hamsters *(Phodopus)*	Longtail dwarfhamsters *(Cricetulus)*	**Common hamsters** *(Cricetus)*	**Golden Hamsters** *(Mesocricetus)*		
Species	Djungarian Hamster *(P. sungorus)*	Roborovski Hamster *(P. roborovskii)*	Chinese Hamster *(C. griseus)*	**European Hamster** *(C. cricetus)*	**Syrian Hamster** *(M. auratus)*	
Subspecies	Dwarf Russian Hamster *(P. s. sungorus)*	Dwarf Russian Campbell's Hamster *(P. s. campbellii)*				

Buying a hamster

Buying a pet is a different matter to buying a toy or a pound of sugar.

Dwarf Russian hamster, pearl

An animal is a living being and we need to treat it well and responsibly. Whether we buy a dog, a cat, a goldfish or a hamster: all our pets depend on us. If we don't feed them, they die. If we don't care for them, they get sick, and if we don't give them a proper home they can escape and, sadly, all too often meet their death in the wild. Taking care of one animal may mean (much) more time than another, but in all cases care is something that must happen every day.

Whenever you're thinking about buying a pet, get all the infor-mation you need in advance. Is this the right animal for your family situation? How much care does it need, and do you have the

time for it over a long period? What does the animal eat, what kind of cage does it need, does it live alone or is it better to have a pair or a group? How much will it cost to buy and look after (including vet's bills) and can you afford that? Get the answers to these questions in advance to avoid disappointments and problems later. If you're in doubt, don't buy the animal!

Before you take your hamster home, you must be sure you have proper accommodation for it (a cage, an aquarium tank or similar in your home. You can't keep a rodent in a cardboard box forever.

If you're buying a hamster for a child, it's important to agree in advance who is going to feed it and keep its home clean. Practice shows that children often promise a lot in their enthusiasm, but don't always keep these promises over time.

You must take account of the fact that a pet needs caring for when you're on holiday or out of the house. The same applies, by the way, when you come home tired after a long day at work or school.

All in all, caring for a pet usually brings lots of pleasure, like having a little piece of nature in your home. And hamsters are excellent as pets. They don't smell, they are relatively easy to care for, and they don't present complications in terms of feeding. Hamsters are moreover almost never aggressive towards humans, which makes them excellent company for children. However, this assumes that the children are not too young. A hamster can hardly defend itself against a toddler's pinching hands.

One or more?
The question of whether one should keep hamsters alone or together is very easy to answer. In the wild some animals live socially, in groups, families or pairs. Others live alone, and that means completely alone. They seek a partner during the breeding period to breed, and then go their own way again. So it's important to keep animals that live alone in the wild alone in captivity too.

Animals that originally lived in groups or pairs are usually happier pets when they have a mate.

The Syrian Hamster lives alone in the wild, so it feels a lot happier when it's alone in captivity too. Hamsters can be very aggressive towards each other and can seriously wound each other, so you should never keep hamsters in a pair or a group.

As an illustration: you buy two young hamsters from the same litter in a pet shop. For a while everything seems fine. But without you noticing, a feud slowly but surely develops between the two animals over time. The stronger

Syrian Hamster

Roborovski Hamster

Professional
rodent stud

Syrian Hamster

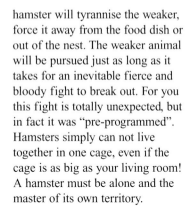

hamster will tyrannise the weaker, force it away from the food dish or out of the nest. The weaker animal will be pursued just as long as it takes for an inevitable fierce and bloody fight to break out. For you this fight is totally unexpected, but in fact it was "pre-programmed". Hamsters simply can not live together in one cage, even if the cage is as big as your living room! A hamster must be alone and the master of its own territory.

Where to buy

You have plenty of options where to buy a hamster. Most hamsters are sold by pet shops, which in itself is a good thing, as generally pet shop owners know how to look after the animals they sell properly. However, there are always some shops that are not so good. You can often spot what kind of a shop you're dealing with. Are the cages clean? Do all the animals have clean water? Are there too many animals in a small tank? Are they selling animals that are wounded or appear sick?

Most pet shops obtain their hamsters from hamster lovers or serious breeders. These animals are healthy and usually used to human hands. A good pet shop owner will also frequently handle his young animals.

Unfortunately, as well as serious breeders and animal lovers, we have our share of rogue breeders in this country. These are people who try to get rich quick by breeding as many hamsters, mice, rabbits or other pets as possible, often keeping the animals in disgusting conditions. They never or hardly ever take care of hygiene, animal welfare is not on their agenda and in-breeding is the order of the day. One of the major disadvantages of these "breeding factories" is that the young are separated from their mother far too early, because time is money after all. The young are nowhere near strong enough and sooner or later become seriously ill. Never buy a hamster (or other pet) that is still too young or too small.

Pets can unfortunately still be found in markets where they are sometimes sold in very questionable conditions; they are often in cages which are far too small and filthy, and are often also far too young. In many cases they are also sick or weak.

However hard it may sound, never give in to the temptation to buy such an animal hoping to give it a better home. You're really not doing any good. The more animals these dealers can sell this way, the more they will keep "in stock". They don't care why you're buying the animal, just as long as you buy it. But if nobody buys their tiny sick animals then they can't make any profit, and they then have to decide either to stop trading or to start taking better care of their animals.

Things to watch out for

If you're planning to buy a hamster, watch out for the following points:

The animal must be healthy. A healthy hamster has bright eyes and is lively. Sexual organs must be clean and the animal must not show signs of wounds or scars. Its coat must be

smooth, clean and glossy. Look out for any lumps or swelling.

Roborovski Hamster

• The hamster must not be too young or too small. During the first weeks of its life the young animal gets resistance to disease through its mother's milk which is vital to its health.

• The animal must also not be too old. Hamsters have a relatively short life. Buying an older animal may mean you will only be able to enjoy it for a short period. Also, adult hamsters are more difficult to tame. You can recognise an older animal by its

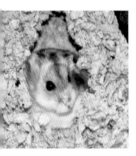

coat, which is somewhat stiffer, and by its yellowish belly.

• Check whether your hamster is really the same sex as the shop assistant tells you. Mistakes are often still made on this point.
• Make sure the animal is neither too thin nor too fat.

Selling young hamsters

However much you like breeding hamsters, sooner or later you can't keep them all. Then you must sell, swap or give away the young.

You can sell young (and older) animals to a pet shop. In this case you never know where they will end up. In any event, look for a serious pet shop that provides broad and correct information when selling animals.

You can also sell the young to private individuals. You might notify a hamster owners' club, place an advertisement in the newspaper or, preferably, sell or give them to acquaintances. Always give the new owner(s) good information about feeding

and caring for hamsters.
Whatever you do, never set
animals loose in the wild. They
will definitely not survive!

Catching and handling

Animals that are not used to being
picked up by human hands are
always frightened by the
experience. Normally, you can
pick up a hamster with one hand,
cupping it with the other hand to
prevent it escaping.
Young animals, especially, have a
tendency to try and jump off your
hand in panic. Hamsters have no
sense of height and will jump
regardless of the height. This is
dangerous and such a fall can
seriously injure such a small
animal. It can even break its back.

When animals are very wild
(which seldom happens with
hamsters) you should use a jam
jar to catch them. It's important to
catch the animal as fast as
possible. Hamsters are not stress-
resistant and a long hunt can
easily upset them and cause
shock.

Transport

When you buy, or are given, a
hamster you have to get the
animal home. In many cases this
is done with a cardboard box. This
is not the best solution. It would
not be the first time (and won't be
the last time either) that a hamster
gnaws a hole in such a box and
goes off on a journey of discovery

in the shopping bag or the car.
So it's better to get a transport
container in advance and you can
buy them at any pet shop. These
containers are too small to be
permanent housing, but very
suitable for the first journey home
or a trip to the vet's. You can also
use it to house your animal
temporarily when you're cleaning
its cage.

Feeding your hamster

Day-in, day-out for years on end, rodents are fed the same thing: mixed rodent food.

However, research into the feeding habits of rodents in the wild has shown that they generally need a quite different and more varied diet.

Feeding in the wild

Very little is known about the Syrian Hamster's feeding habits in its original habitat. Only a few expeditions have been made that found live animals. But we do know about the food eaten by hamsters that roam the wild in Europe. They eat all kinds of plant type produce such as seeds, grain, grasses, fruit and herbs. Besides that they also feed on insects, worms, larvae, snails and even young birds and field mice. This menu varies little from that of the bigger European Hamster and the dwarf hamsters.

Feeding in captivity

When you consider their feeding habits in the wild, it's illogical to feed hamsters only a mixture of oats, grain, barley and grass pellets all the time. These "old-fashioned" foods contained almost no animal content and thus hardly any proteins. So a lot has changed in the field of rodent foods over the last few years.

Major manufacturers have developed special foods for each variety of small rodent. So there are very good foods available, but take care that they contain animal proteins.

Whenever you buy any other food, take care that its structure is not too coarse. Rabbit food is certainly not suitable, nor are grass pellets (in the form of little dark green sticks). If you use mixed rodent food, you can supplement it with dry cat or dog foods, and possibly weed or grass seeds from the bird food shelf.

When buying food, look out for the date of manufacture. The vitamins in the food stay effective for about three months, after which they quickly lose their goodness. Never buy too much food at once.
Just like humans, animals also like variety, but never give rodents sweets, crisps, biscuits or sugar lumps. The salt and sugar these foods contain can make them seriously ill.

If you want to give your hamster a treat once in a while, there are plenty of healthy pet snacks that you can use to put something special on the menu.

Pellets

Pressed pellets
Pet shops also carry ready-made foods in the form of pressed

Rodent snacks

pellets. These pellets all look the same and have the same ingredients. Many breeders give their animals such foods, because then they're sure that each animal gets all the nutrition it needs. Apart from that, a lot less food is wasted as the animals don't pick out what they like best, leaving the rest. But the question is whether they really like getting the same food every day.

Vegetables

Hamsters enjoy most sorts of vegetables, but take care with them. After all, hamsters come from a habitat with very little water (semi-desert) and are not used to large quantities of food with high water content. This can

cause diarrhoea. But now and again they can be treated to a small piece of chicory, endive, carrot, cauliflower, paprika, cucumber or broccoli, but lettuce and cabbage are best left out of their diets.

Fruit

Most rodents, including hamsters, enjoy fruit. What sort is their favourite depends on the animal. Almost every rodent loves apple, pear, peach, raspberries, melon, berries and banana. Most animals find citrus fruits such as oranges and mandarines too sour, but some seem to enjoy them. Just like vegetables, too much of a good thing can be harmful. Take care to remove from the cage any pieces of fruit or vegetables that have not been eaten at once. There is a chance they will start to rot, which could make your hamster ill.

Eating droppings

Almost all rodents eat their own droppings from time to time. This is not only normal, but necessary. During the digestion process, vitamin B12 is produced in the intestines. By eating their droppings the animals take in this important vitamin.

Young hamsters eat their parents' droppings, because they contain the bacteria they need to be able to create vitamin B12 in their own intestines during digestion.

Vitamins and minerals

Vitamins and minerals are elements everybody needs to stay healthy. As long as a hamster enjoys a good, varied diet it does not need additional vitamins and minerals. These are in its food. In the chapter "Your hamster's health" there's more information about the consequences of an unbalanced diet.

Some breeders hang a so-called "mineral lick" in the cage. The animal takes in minerals by licking the stone and it seems that pregnant females, particularly, use them. Sometimes small blocks of limestone are placed in the cage.

By gnawing on these the animals get extra calcium and at the same time keep their teeth sharp.

Water

Many rodents drink only a little water. They come from regions where little water is available and have learned to be careful with it. Some species can go with almost no water at all.
But it's good for a hamster to always have fresh water available. If it's thirsty after all then it can drink at any time. It's best to give water in a drinking bottle as a dish of water is quickly over-turned or filled with shavings or other dirt.

Mineral lick

Water bottle

A home for your hamster

If you want to keep a hamster responsibly and give it a comfortable home, it's important to take a look at how they live in the wild.

Even if your hamster lives in a hutch or a cage at home, it is still possible to get close to their natural living conditions, making the animal feel as comfortable as possible.

In the wild

The hamster that we keep as a house pet originally came from the Middle East. There the landscape consists mainly of savannah and semi-desert. According to data from the Israeli professor Aharoni the Syrian Hamsters that he excavated lived in burrows they dug themselves close to cornfields.

Hamster architecture

Most rodents dig burrows in which to sleep and store their food. Some rodents, such as prairie dogs and chipmunks, build major cavern systems with several entrances. Hamsters spend most of their lives underground, so it goes without saying that they're among the best diggers. Their cavern systems are remarkably extensive and can be several metres deep. This protects them from the enormous differences in temperature that occur in their original habitat. During the day the temperature can be as high as fifty degrees, but at night the temperature can drop to below ten degrees. Deep in the hamster's cavern the temperature will stay fairly constant at around twenty degrees. At dusk, when the temperature has dropped sharply, hamsters will come out to gather their food.

Housing in captivity

So a hamster is a real digger and rooter. It won't be happy living on an old newspaper or a thin layer of sawdust, so a thick floor covering is a must. You need to consider that when choosing a hamster cage. Another aspect you need to consider is that hamsters are masterful escape artists, and they will fiddle at any lock or hook, will gnaw at anything which can be gnawed and climb and hang with enormous strength along wire frames or netting. You can hardly imagine how thin a fat hamster can make itself, let alone what tiny openings it can get through.

But, despite their yearning for freedom, they deserve a comfortable and well looked-after home that should at least fulfil the following conditions:

• their home should keep its residents inside. A poorly closing door, chinks, small holes or too wide a space between bars can be enough. Hamsters can make themselves as thin as a penny.
• their home should be safe for animals and humans. No spikes or other objects, which may harm them, sharp glass edges or lids that fall inward.
• it should be easy to clean, there should be no corners or holes that prevent you from cleaning parts of their home.
• It should be made of a material that won't absorb moisture or smells. Wood is unsuitable for making a pet cage unless it's been treated with a water-repelling coating. When animal urine soaks into wood, it will start to rot and smell. Glass or plastic, on the other hand, are ideal.
• the opening must be wide enough for you to be able to access the entire area of their home. Not just for cleaning purposes but also to be able to catch the animal if necessary. If the door is too small the animal may be able to get into a corner that you can't get at.
• However small your rodent is, its home must be well ventilated. When cage litter is soaked in urine the ammoniac smell can hang around in the bottom of the container. With insufficient ventilation, this can bother the animal.

escape in any direction. The better ones have a small opening for feeding, but you can also open the top leaving the walls standing. Another advantage is that this type of cage is very light and easy to clean.

But a disadvantage is that the base sides are usually low and a burrowing hamster can easily throw sawdust over the edge.

All in all, a wire cage is very suitable if the base is high enough, if it can be opened wide without the animal escaping, and if you can place the cage in an absolutely draught-free place.

Plastic or glass containers
Rodents are frequently kept in old aquariums or plastic containers with a gauze lid. In such a closed container the animals aren't bothered by draughts, but ventilation is not optimal. So you need to clean the cage litter frequently, otherwise the animals live in ammoniac fumes. A lid of glass or plastic sheet is absolutely out of the question because it allows no ventilation at all.

Plastic containers have the disadvantage that they quickly become unsightly, because they are easily scratched. The toilet corner in these containers can also become corroded and rough, making it difficult to keep clean and bad for hygiene.

• There should be areas where the animal can withdraw to in peace.

Types of cages
You can keep your hamster in various types of cages. All have their advantages and disadvantages. Let's look at them one by one:

Wire cage
The majority of cages sold in pet shops are wire cages. They usually consist of a plastic base on which a cage of metal wire sits. The big advantage of this type of cage is their good ventilation: fresh air can get to the animals from all directions. However, a disadvantage is that draughts can do the same.

Some wire cages have a very small opening. If you need a larger opening, then you have to lift the whole top part off the base and your hamster can easily

Glass containers are available in various forms. One-piece containers are easily kept clean, but are also heavy. And if one crack appears you might as well throw it away. There are also aquarium types with a metal frame holding panels of glass. In the past these panels were fixed with putty, which would, of course, not dry out when the aquarium was filled with water. However, old putty tends to crumble in a dry hamster container. The animals can gnaw at it and the panels can become loose. So containers with putty are unsuitable. Nowadays glass panels can be fixed with silicone, which is an easy job for any do-it-yourself enthusiast.

You can also make a glass cage without a frame. The glass panels are glued together with silicone and after one day the container is so strong that you could actually fill it with water. This type of cage can easily and cheaply be made at home. The silicone bead should not be too thick, otherwise the animals will gnaw at it, and the corners should be polished smooth or protected with plastic corner strips, because they can easily cause injury.

Hamster paradise

Pet shops sell pretty, elaborate hamster paradises. Some have a number of wire houses on top of and beside each other, others have a complete burrow system in plastic. Such an exciting hamster home seems ideal to children, of course. But they're not ideal. Some have very narrow corridors and sharp bends where a hamster with a full tummy can easily get stuck, and the plastic tunnels and burrows are difficult to clean and poorly ventilated.

Laboratory pen

Some people keep their hamster in a laboratory pen. These are low plastic containers with a metal grid as a lid. A laboratory container is ideal for housing a lot of animals with the minimum of work, which is the intention in a laboratory. But you have very little contact with the animals. It is also questionable whether they feel happy in such a boring home, and some laboratory pens are so low that a hamster can hardly stand upright inside it.

A box is a very nice playground for your hamster, but not suitable as housing. The hamster will escape very easily.

Hamster paradise pipe

Cage litter

For years, wood shavings have been used in pet cages. They are often called sawdust, but are actually shavings. Shavings absorb moisture exceptionally well and hardly smell, but a disadvantage is that they usually contain a lot of dust. Investigations in recent years have shown that this dust can seriously bother rodents. There are now many other types of cage litter on the market that are "healthier" for animals.

Wood shavings

As we have said, shavings are not especially suitable as cage litter. Now that the dust problem has been generally recognised, some types of shavings are cleaned more thoroughly by the manufacturers. It does appear that animals like the Syrian Hamster, whose natural habitat is dusty and who likes to burrow, are less affected by the dust in wood shavings.

Hay
Rodents like to use hay as nesting material and to chew on, but it does not absorb moisture well and is thus not really suitable as cage litter.

Straw
Straw is much too coarse to be suitable as cage litter or nest material for rodents. There is a product on the market which is made of shredded straw. Some cage litters are wonderfully soft and ideal as nesting material. But they absorb little moisture and are therefore less suitable as cage litter.

Cat litter
There are probably a hundred different sorts of cat litter on the market. Some are suitable to keep rodents on, especially those made from maize. These absorb plenty of moisture and can do good service. Cat litter made of stone or clay is less suitable, mainly because it can become dusty. Cat litter is especially suitable for longhaired hamsters.

Pressed pellets
In recent years various cage litters have appeared on the market that consist of pressed pellets. Some types have sharp edges and don't seem very comfortable.

Sand
Some rodents like to live on sand. But as a floor covering sand has the disadvantage that it doesn't store warmth. Therefore it's unsuitable for hamsters, but if you do choose to use it make sure there's good nesting material available in the cage.

Shredded paper
There are also various types of shredded paper on offer as cage litter. These shreds are ideal to play with and can be used as nest material. But they absorb much too little moisture to be used as cage litter.

In conclusion, use a cage litter that easily absorbs moisture, in combination with a soft, insulating nesting material.

The interior
You can also fit out a hamster's home with various articles from the pet shop. There are literally hundreds of different hamster toys in pet shops. Let's look at the advantages and disadvantages of a number of popular hamster articles:

Hamster houses
There are countless sorts of hamster houses on sale, but most are made of plastic and will be gnawed to destruction within a very short time. Apart from that, most are too small. There are roomier versions, made of wood, which are more suitable for a hamster although they will also gnaw at these.

Wood shavings

Little wood chips

Hay with herbs

Luxury bedding

Cotton wool as
nestling material

Wheels

Opinions vary on the usefulness
of a wheel. Some people insist
that these provide plenty of
recreation for a hamster. That's
surely true, but on the other hand
a wheel does force the animal into
monotonous activity that may
result in psychological
disturbances. The fact is that
hamsters use their wheels a lot,
but they can also cause accidents.
There are no brakes and a
hamster can easily get stuck
between the wheel and its
uprights. Plastic wheels are easy
targets for razor-sharp hamster
teeth.

Straw houses

Hamster houses, tunnels and balls
made of straw have appeared on
the market in recent years. These
products are made of woven straw
and hay held together by wire.
These are ideal toys for hamsters!
They can climb and tunnel in and
around them and gnaw at the
straw and hay. After a while the
straw house is finished with and
you just need to take the wire
skeleton out of the cage.

Climbing ropes

Hamsters love to climb and are
crazy about a climbing rope
suspended from the roof of their
cage. A disadvantage is that the

hamster can easily reach the top of its cage and, especially at night, will hang on the lid and try to gnaw it away.

If you're not keen on ready-made plastic objects, you can fit out your hamster's home really nicely with rocks and twigs, giving it a pretty natural look.

The best place

Take care when picking the place to stand your hamster cage. Places where big temperature differences can occur, such as near an oven or radiator, are not suitable, nor is a window sill which is sometimes in the full sun. Hamsters like to party, but living permanently on top of a loudspeaker is too much of a good thing. The garage or garden shed is also not ideal; after all you want to see your pet from time to time! Apart from that, these places are too quiet, too dark and often too damp.

Preferably place the cage in the living room or a child's bedroom, out of the sun, away from draughts and, where possible, off the ground on a (low) cupboard or table.

Your petshop has a lot of natural houses and toys for your hamster

Behaviour

Hamsters don't speak a
language like humans.
But even if they can't talk,
they do communicate
with each other.

They express their emotions
or intentions (such as readiness
for pairing) with all kinds of non-
verbal communication.

Scents, sounds
and body-talk

Hamsters often rub their flanks
along objects to leave their scent.
That way other hamsters know
they have to keep out of the area.
A female ready to mate gives off
another scent so that males know
she's looking for a mating
partner.

The most important means of
communication between hamsters
however is body talk. A hamster
that stretches itself, yawns and
sits washing itself carefully feels
comfortable. But if it washes
itself with rapid movements this

is a diversionary tactic; it doesn't
know how to handle the situation.
If it rolls itself up with its muzzle
pointed diagonally upwards, then
it's frightened. If a hamster lays
on its back on the ground this
signifies fear, subjection, but also
a readiness to defend itself. If it
should actually be attacked, all
the means of defence at its
disposal (paws and snout) can
easily be put into action.

When a hamster attacks it usually
gets up on its hind legs. It will
try to bite and strike with its
forepaws.

You won't often hear a hamster,
but they do possess a range of
sounds, from screeches and
hissing to little squeaking noises.
They only screech when in a

fierce fight or when under attack by an enemy (like the cat). These screams can be very impressive. They open their mouth wide and their teeth are pointed forward as a threat.

Young animals squeak loudly when they wake up hungry and, by chance, their mother is not in the area.

House-training

In principle, most rodents are house-trained by nature. They don't like to foul their own nest and will always do their business in the same corner of their home. This can be practical because sometimes it won't be necessary to clean out the whole cage, but just to scrape out the "toilet corner".

Cuddling your hamster

When keeping a hamster as a pet, it's important that it's tame (as far as possible).
This not only helps when you clean out its cage, or when it needs to be (medically) examined, but it's fun too. You can even play with it. Tame hamsters enjoy being picked up once in a while, but these little animals are not suitable to be cuddled for hours at a time; they don't like it and can get frightened. If you're looking for a cuddly animal, go to a toyshop.

Hamsters try to put almost anything into their cheek pouches.

Defence position

This is a dangerous situation! The dog could bite the hamster, but the hamster could just as easily bite the dog in its nose.

Taming the hamster

When taming a hamster you can exploit its natural curiosity. When something unusual happens, it will run for cover, but after a while a plucky hero will reappear. Hold your hand in the cage with something tasty on it and, sooner or later, the hamster will approach it. But don't try to catch the animal at once, because you'll destroy the newly-won trust. Let the hamster get used to the scent of your hand and then sit on it.

After a few attempts, you can carefully lift your hand a little. The hamster will get more and more comfortable with it. Never chase after your animal, it will only get frightened. Hungry animals are easier to train with something tasty than an animal that's just eaten, so always do your taming exercises before you feed your hamster. Taming a hamster can sometimes require patience, so don't give up too fast if you don't get immediate results.

Shows

Hobby breeders also breed hamsters. Just like dogs, cats, rabbits, chickens and pigeons that are put on show and compete for points.

Hamster lovers have several cages with hamsters at home and try to breed particularly fine examples. During shows, which may be one day or more, each animal is judged. A so-called "standard" exists for every known variety and colouring, which describes exactly how each variant should look. The Syrian Hamster is a recognised species that can be entered for a show. During the show an expert judge evaluates each animal in terms of size, colour, shape and condition. If you're interested in taking up this hobby you can contact the National Hamster Council (see the chapter on "Clubs"). Even if you're not planning to start breeding, but are simply interested in rodents, it's worth taking the trouble to visit a small animal show.

You can pick up a lot of information there, and often the breeders present have good animals for sale.

Colours and hairstyles

The original (Syrian) hamster had a splendid, golden-brown coat, which is why it was called the "Golden Hamster". Spontaneous mutations and (later) deliberate breeding produced many different colourings. For hobby breeding some of these colourings have been laid down in writing and recognised as standards. There are countless other colour mixes which are not recognised. These are known as "floaters". Hamsters can also have different "hairstyles", where the structure of their coat differs from the shorthaired hamster.

Coat structures

The shorthaired coat is the "standard" coat structure for hamsters. This coat is also known as smooth-coated or normal-coated. It is short, woolly and soft. The satin-haired hamster possesses a pretty glossy coat. The gloss is a result of the fact that the hairs are hollow. This coat is also short and soft, but may not be woolly.

From the United States comes the longhaired hamster. The male's hair is five to eight centimetres long, the female's three to four centimetres. Longhaired hamsters appear to pull their coat behind them.
Pet shops often sell crosses of long and short-coated hamsters, because these animals look so cuddly. But among show breeders these are regarded as "failures".

A special hairstyle is worn by the Rex, or curly-coated hamster. This variety has a short, thick coat with little curls. A special feature of this coat structure is its curly whiskers.

Colours

As already discussed, hamsters come in very many different colours. It would be going too far to describe them all in this book. If you'd like to know more, you can consult the breed standards at the National Hamster Council. In this chapter we will restrict ourselves to a few characteristic colourings.
A white hamster is often wrongly referred to as an albino. An albino has absolutely no pigments; it is colourless. Real albinos always have red eyes and flesh-coloured ears. In the wild

White pink-eyed

Crème satin

Black

these spontaneous mutations have little chance of survival.

With hamsters, we differentiate between the white red-eyed and the white black-eyed varieties. The white red-eyed does have red eyes but dark grey ears. The white black-eyed has black eyes. Therefore neither variety is an albino!

A frequent hamster colour is crème. A perfect crème hamster displays a warm creamy colour and red or black eyes.

Close to the crème colouring come the beige, blonde, yellow, copper and orange colourings. These colours are either lighter or darker than crème and more or less mixed with red.

The sepia variety has also been around for a long time. This is a strongly blended colour, with grey, brown and black hairs. There are light and dark sepia varieties. The light sepia hamster's main colour is grey, the dark sepia's dark brown. Black hamsters are a recent addition of the past few years. Breeders had to work hard to create this colour. Especially over the past few years, more and more colourings seem to have been bred. They often have elegant and descriptive names such as silver, sable, honey, smoke pearl, mink, ivory, guinea gold, champagne, chocolate, caramel and dove-grey.

Crème

Markings
Apart from single-coloured hamsters there are also animals with two or three colours. They possess a so-called marking. Almost all marked hamsters have a white base colour. Only the tortoiseshell hamster has a yellow base colour.

The white-band possesses a belted marking; a white band rings its body. The tri-colour has white and yellow spots mixed with a third colour such as black, gold or orange. There are also multicoloured, or spotted hamsters.

Dwarf hamsters

Everyone knows hamsters, but the dwarf hamster is less well known, despite the fact that these mini-hamsters have been kept as pets for some twenty-five years. We shouldn't really talk of the dwarf hamster as such because there are many species.

Dwarf Russian hamster

This book covers only the species that are kept as pets in this country. These are the Dwarf Russian Hamster, the Dwarf Campbell's Russian Hamster, the Chinese Hamster and the Roborovski Dwarf Hamster. Dwarf hamsters are closely related to "normal" hamsters, but one cannot simply class them as "little hamsters". They vary in many respects, and there are even major differences among the dwarf hamsters themselves.

The Dwarf Russian hamster

The Dwarf Russian hamster, also known as the Djungarian Dwarf Hamster, originates from the steppes of Northern Kazakhstan and Siberia. These steppes form a hostile region to the north of China. The name "Russian" is

actually incorrect, as the animal is never found in true Russia. In 1968, the first four examples were caught in Western Siberia and brought to the Max Planck Institute in Germany for investigation. The animals seemed to reproduce extremely easily in captivity. At the beginning of the seventies the first animals arrived in this country and were soon followed by other examples that found their way here via various Eastern European institutes.

To the scientist, the Dwarf Russian hamster lives its life under the Latin name *Phodopus sungorus sungorus*. Thus scientists across the world know which animal is referred to, whatever language they speak.

The Rus is a small, ball-shaped animal whose coat is less woolly than that of the Dwarf Campbell's Russian hamster. Its back is grey-brown with a striking wide and darker dorsal stripe. Its belly is white or light grey with a somewhat darker (blue) undercoat. The border between its dark back and lighter underside is a black-brown line that runs in three bows. The Rus has deep black eyes.

A Dwarf Russian hamster that is not kept indoors gets a beautiful white winter coat. This is a natural protective colour during a period when its original habitat is covered in snow. The colour change results not from a drop in temperature, but due to the shortening days, i.e. under the influence of light. The soles of its feet are fur covered, to protect them from the cold Siberian ground.

Apart from the normal wild colouring, the Rus can also be found in the colours pearl and sapphire (a natural blue colouring). If you come across a dwarf hamster in any other colour, it's definitely not a Rus, but possibly a Campbell's or a cross between a Rus and a Campbell's.

The Campbell's Russian hamster
The Campbell's Russian hamster is closely related to the Dwarf Russian hamster. They can be crossbred, although this is not good for the preservation of the two sub-species. Animals born of such pairings often struggle with health and behaviour problems (aggression). The Campbell's Russian hamster originates from the more easterly steppes, mainly in the north of Mongolia and China.

Dwarf Russian hamster

Because of its thicker coat the Campbell's appears somewhat larger than the Dwarf Russian hamster, but in fact it's not. Campbell's tend to become fatter in captivity than the Russian. The Campbell's coat is yellow-brownish with a thin, sharply lined dorsal stripe. Its coat turns slightly greyer in winter, but not to the extent of its Russian cousin. The Campbell's feet also have fur covered soles.

The Campbell's first came to Britain in 1964, also arriving here from a scientific institute where they were first used as experimental animals. They were later exported to other countries.

Campbell's Russian hamster

The Latin name for the Campbell's Russian hamster is *Phodopus sungorus campbellii*. The first two parts of a Latin name specify the species. The Russian and the Campbell's thus belong to the same species as they both carry the name *Phodopus sungorus*. The third

part of the Latin name specifies the sub-species, and here we see the difference between the two species (*sungorus* and *campbellii*). In contrast to the Dwarf Russian hamster, the Campbell's has been bred in a whole range of different colours. The original colourings were white and argente (yellow-light brown). The argente variety is similar in colour to the Roborovski Dwarf Hamster. There are also Campbell's with a satin coat structure. "Show" breeders are always working hard to create new colour variations.

The Roborovski Hamster

The Roborovski Hamster (*Phodopus roborovskii*) is also a short-tailed dwarf hamster, but its yellow-brown colouring and striking whiskers lend it a totally different appearance to the other two short-tailed species. The Roborovski Dwarf Hamster's original habitat is in western and southern Mongolia, a dry and barren region of many semi-deserts. Dwarf hamsters do not inhabit true deserts.

Although Robbys have been around longer than Campbell's, they are much less well known. The reason is that Roborovskis bred very few young, especially in the early years in this country. In the wild a female will bear only two or three litters in her life. As time moved on, the

Roborovskis adapted to life in captivity and now they also breed more young. But the Roborovski remains a seldom seen variety. The Roborovski Hamster is the smallest dwarf hamster. Its body measures only seven to nine centimetres in length and its tail is barely visible. Its back is a brownish-yellow with grey undercolouring. Sometimes the yellow on its back appears somewhat rusty in colour. Robbys don't have the dorsal stripe of other dwarf hamsters. Its eyes are jet-black with white spots above them, which look like eyebrows. Its belly is a smooth white colour.

Roborovski Hamster

Chinese Hamster

The Chinese Hamster

The Chinese Hamster is a long-tailed dwarf hamster and not

Dwarf Russian hamster

closely related to the other three species. This is also apparent from its Latin name *Cricitulus griseus*, which is totally different from the others. The Chinese Hamster comes from northern China where it lives on the steppes and can be found in woods as well as in populated areas. Chinese Hamsters have been kept in captivity more than thirty years. In earlier years they were the dwarf hamster variety most frequently seen at rodent shows, but today they are less common.

That the Chinese is not directly related to the other dwarf hamsters can be seen from its appearance. Most striking is its build and the tail. The other dwarf hamsters are small, round balls without a tail, while the Chinese has an elongated body shape and a clearly visible tail. The Chinese Hamster's coat is not as woolly as that of the other species. Its fur lies close and smooth on the skin. The coat is grey-brown in colour with very fine, black spots, which are known as "ticking". The thin dark-brown dorsal stripe on its back is not always clearly visible and its belly is light grey. The Chinese hamster has dark ears, lightly edged. The difference between male and female is easy to spot: the male has a strikingly large scrotum.

Since the beginning of the eighties, spotted Chinese have also appeared. This colour mutation was achieved in Britain and has a strange genetic side-effect: some of the young die in the womb. White Chinese with a dark dorsal stripe were bred in Switzerland at the University of Zurich. This mutation also has a

genetic surprise: the males stay sterile.

One or more?

The question of whether one should keep dwarf hamsters alone or together is not easy to answer. All dwarf hamsters, except the Chinese, live in groups in the wild. So as pets they feel happier in a group or with their partner. So it's important to know what kind of hamster you've got. Chinese hamsters can be very difficult towards each other and can cause themselves serious bite wounds. You should never keep this variety of hamster as a pair or in

Dwarf Russian
Campbell's hamster

Roborovski Hamster

Roborovski
Hamster

a group! The other three species are happier when they have company. Indeed, the Campbell's tends to become lazy and fat when it's kept alone.

If you keep two or more dwarf hamsters of the opposite sex together, then sooner or later you can expect family additions. That first nestful of baby dwarf hamsters is, of course, real sweet and you can usually find homes for them quickly among neighbours, friends and the children's friends. But when you have a nestful a couple of times a year, your friends have soon all been supplied, and it gets more difficult to find good homes for the young.

Birth control is not a simple matter with such small animals as dwarf hamsters, so to avoid being overrun by hamsters it's better to keep males and females apart. However, if you do want to breed a nest of young at some time, it can be difficult putting a grown male and female together (see the chapter on "Reproduction").
If you do plan to keep a pair or a group of dwarf hamsters, it's best to buy young animals of the same sex. This almost never causes problems.

Which species?

Of the four species of dwarf hamsters that are sold as pets in this country, some are found more often than others. They're almost never sold at the same time. Unfortunately the staff at many pet stores often don't know exactly what variety of dwarf hamster they are selling. Mostly these are Russian or Campbell's dwarf hamsters or a cross of the two species. These are all friendly, good-natured animals that love company and enjoy being stroked.

The Roborovski Hamster is particularly pretty. It looks wonderful with its large whiskers and is somewhat livelier, but a Robby is something to watch rather than to cuddle.

Chinese Hamsters get on well with humans, but can be very aggressive towards other dwarf hamsters and other small animals. They must definitely be kept alone.

Reproductic

As hamsters cannot live in groups or pairs, they can never surprise you with babies, which is not the case for other rodents. Breeding hamsters is a deliberate choice.

You need to know in advance whether the young have a good home to go to, because they must be separated from the mother in six weeks or so. You can ask your pet shop whether they need young hamsters or perhaps neighbours, friends or acquaintances will take them.

Should you be left with young, then you must find another, perhaps less pleasant, way to deal with them, because they really must not be kept in the cage with their mother. One solution, of course, is to go out and buy another six to eight cages as homes for the youngsters, but this is not an option for many people. So only start to breed if you've found good homes for the young!

Male or female?
To breed hamsters, you first need to be sure that you have a male and a female available. With hamsters the difference between the sexes cannot be seen at a glance. You have to examine them closely under the tail.

As with most rodents, you can tell the sex of a hamster from the space between its anus and its genital opening. This distance is much larger on males than on females. On grown males you can also detect the shape of the scrotum.

Pairing
When the time is right for breeding you must bring the male and female together. This is called "pairing".

Pairing hamsters is no easy matter. The female will only accept the male close by when she is ready to mate, which is only once every four days. The only way to find out which days those are is to simply try. Always put the female into the male's cage or put them together in neutral territory. The female will never accept the male in her cage, even if she is ready to mate.

Because hamsters are dusk or nocturnal animals, mating is best done in the evening. Two things might happen when you put the female in with the male.

There is a 75% chance that the female will immediately attack the male. Obviously, she is not ready to mate. Use a piece of thick cardboard or a wooden panel to separate the animals. Never do this with your hands, the female will go for your fingers too! The following evening you can try again and just keep trying until the female lets the male come to her.

If the female is fertile, she will stand stock-still, with a straight back and raised tail waiting for the male.

In-breeding
To breed responsibly, you must only ever use strong, healthy adult animals. And you may never put any male together with any

female, because there is a high risk of in-breeding. For instance, if you've been given a brother and sister from a neighbour's litter, it's better not to mate them. Pairing these animals is a serious form of in-breeding, and who can guarantee that your neighbour's litter was not also the result of pairing a brother and sister?

For many animal species, in-breeding is a disaster for the population. Syrian Hamsters are somewhat less sensitive in this respect, evidenced by the fact that the whole population of hamsters in captivity today stems from just a few animals. One instance of in-breeding is certainly not a disaster with Syrian Hamsters, but if it happens frequently the results do become apparent. Young born from in-breeding get smaller and weaker each litter; the litters become smaller and smaller in number and, finally, young are born with in-born mutations.

Mating
Before mating actually occurs the male sniffs and licks the female and then mates with her several times, washing himself quickly in-between. Some inexperienced animals try to mate with the female at the wrong end (the head). You can easily correct this. The female gives the male between fifteen and thirty minutes to mate. Then she becomes active again and the male needs to get away

quickly. This is the time to remove the female from the cage again. Normally the female is now pregnant, but occasionally things go wrong for various reasons. In the cold dark winter months, mating fails more often than during the rest of the year. It can also happen that one of the adult animals is too old or infertile. Animals that are too fat are more likely to be infertile.

Pregnancy and birth

Hamster pregnancies are short and generally result in few problems. Sometimes you can hardly see that the female is pregnant, but if she's carrying a lot of young, she will become as round as a ball. The young are born about 16 days after mating. Leave the pregnant female in peace as much as possible. Give her extra nutritious food, especially proteins in the form of dog or cat biscuits. As the

cage cannot be cleaned during the first three weeks after the birth, this is best done just beforehand.

Immediately before the birth the female becomes very restless, she fetches enormous amounts of nesting material. Give the mother-to-be plenty of extra nesting material in the form of shredded kitchen paper or cloth. Never use synthetic materials such as cotton wool as the young can get tangled up in it.

The birth itself normally takes place in the afternoon or evening and is over quickly and without problems. As the young are born, they start to squeak loudly and their mother licks them clean.

The size of a litter can vary from just one baby to as many as fifteen. On average six to eight young are born. In some

cases babies may be rejected. The mother does this for a reason. Usually the baby concerned is sick or unlikely to survive for other reasons. Sometimes an inexperienced mother will leave her young lying around all over the cage, especially if she's been disturbed. NEVER pick these young up with your bare hands! Leave the mother and her offspring in peace and she will normally collect her young herself. If she doesn't, then after some time lay the young back into the nest using toilet paper or some other soft material.

Development

At birth the young weigh approximately two grams, and they are naked, blind and completely helpless. They look like small pink shrimps. The first signs of fur and markings appear after a couple of days, and after almost two weeks they open their eyes and can also hear. Before that, they slowly start to nibble at food, and after three weeks they are totally self-sufficient. They stop taking milk from their mother after eighteen to twenty days.

The following weeks are called the "flea age". The young become totally restless and dart around, but they calm down again when they're about five weeks old, when they can also be separated from the mother.

Your hamster's health

Fortunately, hamsters generally have few health problems. A healthy example has bright eyes and is lively. Its coat is smooth, soft and regular. Its rear body is dry and clean.

A sick hamster sits withdrawn all the time. Its coat is dull and stands open, as if wet. The animal's back is raised, even when walking.

Prevention
The rule that "prevention is better than a cure" also applies to small animals such as the hamster. It's not always easy to cure a sick hamster. They are so small that even a vet doesn't always know how to treat them.

Even a light cold can prove fatal for a hamster and the biggest risks to its health are draughts and damp.

There are a few general rules that you can follow if your hamster is ill:

- Keep the animal in a quiet semi-dark place. Stress, crowding and noise won't help it get better.
- Keep the animal warm, but make sure its surroundings are not too hot. The best temperature is 20 to 21 degrees.
- Don't wait too long before visiting a vet. Small rodents that get sick usually die within a few days.
- The patient should always have fresh water and remember that your pet may be too weak to reach its water bottle.
- Sick animals often eat little or nothing. Give it a small piece of apple or other fruit.

Colds and pneumonia
Draughts are the most common cause of colds and pneumonia for hamsters, so choose the place for its home carefully.

They can withstand low temperatures, but cold in combination with a draught almost inevitably leads to a cold. The hamster starts sneezing and gets a wet nose. If its cold gets worse, the animal starts to breathe with a rattling sound and its nose will run even more, so it's now high time to visit the vet, who can prescribe antibiotics. A hamster with a cold or pneumonia must be kept in a draught-free and warm room (22 to 25 degrees).

Diarrhoea

Diarrhoea is another formidable threat to hamsters and often ends fatally. Unfortunately, diarrhoea is usually the result of incorrect feeding, sometimes in combination with draughts or damp. Most cases of diarrhoea are caused by giving the animal food with too high a moisture content. After all, the hamster by nature is a seed and herb eater. Rotten\ food or dirty drinking water can also be a cause. You can do a lot to prevent diarrhoea.

But should your hamster become a victim then you must take any moist food out of the cage immediately. Feed your animal only dry bread, boiled rice or crispbread. Replace its water with lukewarm camomile tea. Clean

Deficiency of	Symptoms	Found in
Protein	Poor coat, hair loss, pneumonia, infertility and poor growth of young animals, aggression (both with too much and too little)	Peas, beans, soya, cheese
Vitamin A	Pneumonia, damage to mucous membrane or eyes, growth problems, diarrhoea and general infections, cramps, small litters	Root vegetables, egg-yolk, fresh greens, bananas and other fruit, cheese
Vitamin B complex	Hair loss, reduced fertility, weight loss, trembling, nervous symptoms, anaemia, infections	Oat flakes, greens, fruit, clover, dog biscuits, grains
Vitamin C	The hamster produces this itself, deficiency rarely a problem Growth problems, poor bone condition	Greens, fruit
Vitamin D	Too much vitamin D causes calcium loss in bones and calcium deposits in blood vessels	Dairy products, egg-yolk
Vitamin E	Infertility, muscle infections, nervous problems, bleeding and poor growth of young animals	Egg-yolk, sprouting grains, fresh grains, greens
Vitamin K	(Nose) bleeding, poor healing of wounds and growth problems.	Greens
Calcium	Normally produced in the animal's intestines. Lameness, calcium loss in bones and broken teeth	Mineral preparations, dairy products, sepia, varied diet
Potassium	Weight loss, heart problems and ascitis, wetness in open abdominal cavity	Fruit
Sodium	Can only occur with serious diarrhoea	Cheese, varied diet
Magnesium	Restlessness, irritability, cramps, diarrhoea and hair loss	Greens, grains
Iron	Anaemia, stomach and intestinal disorders, infertility	Greens, grains, meat
Iodine	Metabolic disorders and thyroid gland abnormalities	Greens, grains, water

out its cage litter and nest material twice a day. As soon as the patient is completely recovered, you must disinfect its cage.

Wet tail

E-coli bacteria cause an especially serious form of diarrhoea and most victims die within 48 hours. Hamsters that fall victim to this disease have a constantly wet tail and anus; they won't eat and become apathetic.

E-coli bacteria are normally present in small quantities in the intestines of a small rodent. In the event of reduced resistance or stress the bacteria suddenly become active. Whenever your hamster has a wet tail take it to the vet's immediately.

Tumours

In contrast to most other rodents, hamsters seldom have problems with tumours, and when they do this is mostly in old age. Tumours occur more frequently in strains where in-breeding has occurred, in other words where animals have been crossed with their own family members. The most common tumours affect the female's teats, but tumours can also be the result of skin cancer. These forms can be operated on but, because of the animal's age, this rarely makes sense.

Another form of tumour is caused by infections under the skin,

which is called an abscess. A small wound may heal, but an infection remains under the skin. This type of tumour can be easily treated by the vet who opens and cleans it. Should your hamster show signs of a tumour, take it straight to the vet's. Delaying can only make things worse, both with skin cancer and abscesses.

Bite wounds

The most common injuries suffered by a hamster are the result of fights. Pairing adult animals is not always easy and can sometimes result in fierce fighting.

Bite wounds generally heal quickly, and as long as they're not

too big or too deep you usually don't need to do much. Don't let the wounded animal sit on shavings or sand for the first few days. Small pieces might get into the wound. Shredded paper or kitchen roll is a good alternative.

Broken bones

Hamsters sometimes break bones because they get stuck with their paws, jump off your hand or fall from a table. An animal with a broken paw will not put weight on it and will limp around the cage. If it's a "straight" fracture (the paw is not deformed), this will heal within a few weeks. Take care that the hamster can reach its food and drink without difficulty. If a hamster has broken its back, it's best to have it put to sleep. If in doubt about a possible fracture, always ask your vet.

Broken teeth

Hamsters that are fed an unbalanced diet with too few minerals run the risk of broken teeth. If you notice that your hamster has a broken tooth, check that its diet is properly balanced. The vet can prescribe gistocal tablets to restore the calcium level. A broken front tooth will normally grow back, but you should check regularly that this is happening.

Overgrown teeth

A rodent's front teeth grow continuously and are ground down regularly by its gnawing. A genetic defect, a heavy blow or lack of gnawing opportunities can disrupt this process. Its teeth are ground irregularly and in the end don't fit together properly. In some cases the teeth continue to grow unchecked, even into the opposite jaw. When a rodent's teeth are too long, it can no longer chew properly and the animal will lose weight and eventually starve to death. Long teeth can easily be clipped back. A vet can show you how to do that, or do it for you if you don't feel able. Take care that your rodent always has enough to gnaw on. A piece of breeze block, a block of wood or a branch will do fine.

Malnutrition ailments

Not only calcium deficiency, but also a shortage of other minerals and vitamins can lead to sick-

nesses. See the table on page 58 for an overview of sicknesses that can arise from certain deficiencies.

Parasites

Parasites are small creatures that live at the cost of their host. The best known are fleas on dogs and cats. Rodents seldom have problems with parasites, and certainly not healthy animals. Weak, sick or poorly cared-for animals, however, are far more likely to be affected. You mostly discover parasites only when an animal starts to scratch itself and gets bald patches. If you notice that your hamster is itching and scratches itself frequently, then it's probably suffering from lice (tiny spiders that feed on blood).

Hamsters have yellow teeth, like most rodents

These lice are often spread by birds, and hamsters sometimes pick up a flea from a dog or cat. A pet shop or vet can advise you on dealing with parasites.

Skin mites

The skin mite is a particularly harmful parasite. Fortunately they seldom occur but if they affect your hamster, you've got work to do. The skin mite is a minute spider that creeps into its host's skin, making the mite itself almost never visible. It causes scabs and eczema, which sometimes cover the whole skin within a month. Skin mites are infectious and can be passed on to other animals.

Your vet or a good pet shop will have treatments for skin mites. Read the instructions on the packaging thoroughly. In most cases the infected animal must be bathed in the substance. Dry your hamster off well to prevent it catching a cold and put it in a warm place (minimum 25 degrees).

Fungal skin infections

Rodents can sometimes suffer from fungal skin infections, which cause small areas of flaking in the ears or nose. Skin fungi are infectious to humans and animals but easy to treat. But don't let the problem go on too long because the animal may suffer other ailments because of it. Your vet has standard medicines against fungi.

Old age

Obviously we hope that your hamster will grow old without disease and pain. However, hamsters live nowhere near as long as humans and you must reckon with the fact that after a couple of years you have an old hamster to care for. Such an old hamster will slowly become quieter and get grey hair in its coat, and now it needs a different kind of care. The time for wild games is over; it won't like them anymore. Leave your hamster in peace. In the last few weeks and days of its life, you will notice its fur decaying and the animal will get thinner. Don't try to force it to eat if it doesn't want to; the end is usually not long off. Hamsters, on average, live only two years. A three-year old hamster is very old, and only in exceptional cases do they reach the age of four.

Mite

Clubs

Becoming a member of a club can be very useful for good advice and interesting activities.

Midland Hamster Club
www.midlandhamsterclub.co.uk/
Sec. Elaine Skidmore
Email: bchams@talk21.com

The Northern Ireland Hamster Club
Sec. Rachel Cooper
4 Rusheyhill Road, Lisburn, Co. Antrim, BT28 3TD.
Tel: 028 9264 8133
Email: secretary@nihc.org.uk
www.nihc.org.uk

Heart of England Hamster Club
E-mail: flordon@aol.com

Northern Hamster Club
www.hamsterpage.ic24.net
Email: sandra.n.h.c@ic24.net

The Hamster Society
The Membership Secretary
3 Laverockdale Loan,
Edinburgh EH13 0EZ
United Kingdom
E-mail: grant@hamsoc.org.uk
www.forrestg.pwp.blueyonder.co.uk

The National Hamster Council
PO box 154
Rotherham
South Yorkshire
S66 OFL UK
E-mail:
hamstercouncil@bigfood.com
www.hamsters-uk.org

Internet

A great deal of information can be found on the internet. A selection of websites with interesting details and links to other sites and pages is listed here. Sometimes pages move to another site or address. You can find more sites by using the available search engines.

www.towyvale.com
On this pages you will find lots of information about hamsters. They list all the UK hamster clubs, many hamster clubs from other countries plus known hamster shows in the UK. Information leaflets on many aspects of hamster keeping and a hamster FAQ.

www.petwebsite.com/hamsters.asp
Loads of colour photographs, information on breeding, genetics, housing and just about anything that is remotely concerned with hamsters.

www.geocities.com/dustywug
Make sure you put your extreme colour eye protection on before visiting this site!

www.minxlinx.co.uk
Hamster links from around the world

www.smallandfurries.co.uk
Information on Roborovski, Russian and Mouse-like hamsters is contained.

www.rodentrefuge.co.uk
The Refuge is based in the Northeast of England and is a permanent place for pet rodents that need a new place to live. All rodents that come into the Refuge stay at the Refuge for the rest of their lives and are treated with love and care, as all pets should be.

www.hamsterland.com
Lots of general hammy info.

The hamster

Name:	Syrian Hamster
Latin name:	*Mesocrisetus auratus*
Origin:	Syria
Body length:	12-16 cm
Tail length:	9-14 mm
Weight:	120-180 grams
Body temperature:	37-38 degrees
Fertile age:	4-5 weeks
Ready for breeding:	3-4 months (male), 4-6 months (female)
Stop breeding:	18-24 months (male), 12 months (female)
Menstrual cycle:	4 days
Term of pregnancy:	16 days
Number of young:	1-15 (average 6-8)
Birth weight:	2 grams
Eyes open:	after approximately 14 days
Suckling time:	18-20 days
Average life expectancy:	2-3 years (max. 4 years)
Food intake:	10-20 grams per day
Ambient temperature:	13-20 °C